THAT'S MY JAM!

HIP-HOP MUSIC

BY NATHAN SOMMER

EUREKA!, AN IMPRINT OF BELLWETHER MEDIA BY FLUTTERBEE

eureka!

Eureka! books turn real stories into unforgettable experiences. Clear, direct language and sharp, captivating imagery make it easy to follow your curiosity, one fascinating fact at a time. Your Eureka! moment awaits!

This edition first published in 2027 by Bellwether Media, Inc.

For information regarding permission, write to Bellwether Media, Inc., Attention: Permissions Department, 3500 American Blvd W, Suite 150, Bloomington, MN 55431.

Library of Congress Cataloging-in-Publication Data

Names: Sommer, Nathan author
Title: Hip-hop music / by Nathan Sommer.
Description: Eureka. | Minneapolis : Bellwether Media, Inc, 2027. | Series: That's my jam! | Includes index. | Audience: Ages 9-13 | Audience: Grades 7-9 | Summary: ""Engaging images accompany information on hip-hop music. The text level and subject matter are intended for students in grades 5 through 9"-Provided by publisher"-- Provided by publisher.
Identifiers: LCCN 2026001576 (print) | LCCN 2026001577 (ebook) | ISBN 9798898801250 (library binding) | ISBN 9798898802493 (ebook)
Subjects: LCSH: Rap (Music)--History and criticism
Classification: LCC ML3531 .S667 2027 (print) | LCC ML3531 (ebook) | DDC 782.421649--dc23/eng/20260128

Editor: Elizabeth Neuenfeldt   Series Designer: Josh Brink

Printed in the United States of America, North Mankato, MN.

TABLE OF CONTENTS

WHAT IS HIP-HOP? 4
THE HISTORY OF HIP-HOP 6
HIP-HOP TIMELINE 10
INSTRUMENTS 12
AWARDS AND HONORS 14
TYPES OF HIP-HOP 16
HIP-HOP PROFILES 20
THE FUTURE OF HIP-HOP 44
GLOSSARY 46
WRITE ABOUT IT! 47
INDEX 48

WHAT IS HIP-HOP?

Hip-hop features rhymed, spoken words. They are recorded over strong beats. Artists often use samples from other songs to make new sounds. Hip-hop is more than a genre. It is a culture that includes rapping, dancing, DJing, and creating art. Songs tell stories of community and social issues. They also celebrate success and overcoming struggles.

DRAKE

BEHIND THE NAME

Many believe Keith Wiggins created the term *hip-hop* in the 1970s. He used the word to describe the sound of marching soldiers.

Hip-hop subgenres include trap and boom bap. Latin hip-hop and pop hip-hop are also popular. Drake, Kendrick Lamar, and Bad Bunny are some of hip-hop's biggest stars today.

THE HISTORY OF HIP-HOP

Hip-hop culture began in the 1970s. It started in New York City's Bronx neighborhood. DJ Kool Herc used turntables to blend music at block parties. Artists began adding funk and soul elements to create new beats. They started rapping over these beats. People developed breakdancing as a way to move to the new sounds.

HIP-HOP AND GRAFFITI

Graffiti art was a big part of early hip-hop. Artists used spray paint and markers. They created graffiti on buildings, bridges, and trains.

DJ KOOL HERC

BEASTIE BOYS

RUN-DMC

Sugarhill Gang released "Rapper's Delight" in 1979. It was hip-hop's first major hit. Run-DMC and the Beastie Boys soon made hip-hop popular worldwide. They made faster beats and used drums to create rap rock.

Rivalries between West Coast and East Coast rappers ruled 1990s hip-hop. This led to the rise of gangsta rap. Queen Latifah and Lil' Kim opened new doors for female rappers.

LIL' KIM

QUEEN LATIFAH

THE FIRST HIP-HOP GRAMMY

The Grammys formed the Best Rap Performance category in 1989. DJ Jazzy Jeff & The Fresh Prince won that year. They earned it for their song "Parents Just Don't Understand."

Hip-hop had a futuristic sound during the 2000s. Southern artists such as OutKast and Ludacris also became popular. Trap music soon took over. Today, Drake and Bad Bunny blend different genres. They blur the line between rapper and pop star.

HIP-HOP TIMELINE

1973
DJ Kool Herc holds his first block party, which many consider to be the birth of hip-hop

1979
"Rapper's Delight" by the Sugarhill Gang becomes hip-hop's first hit

1987
Licensed to Ill by the Beastie Boys becomes the first rap album to reach number one

DJ KOOL HERC

1986
The "Walk This Way" rock-rap collaboration between Aerosmith and Run-DMC helps bring hip-hop into the mainstream

1989
The first Grammy for Best Rap Performance is awarded

RUN-DMC WITH AEROSMITH

EMINEM

2003

Eminem becomes the first hip-hop artist to win an Oscar for his movie *8 Mile*

BAD BUNNY

2022

Bad Bunny's *Un Verano Sin Ti* is the year's best-selling album in the U.S., a major success for Latin hip-hop

1990s

The rivalry between East Coast and West Coast artists grows

2018

Kendrick Lamar becomes the first hip-hop artist to win a Pulitzer Prize

2005

Lil Wayne creates Young Money Entertainment, the group that launches Drake and Nicki Minaj into superstardom

LIL WAYNE

INSTRUMENTS

TURNTABLES

Turntables helped create hip-hop. They use needles to turn grooves on records into sound waves. They help DJs remix and extend songs in real time.

DRUM MACHINES

Drum machines replace live drumming. They make many of hip-hop's powerful beats and rhythms. The Roland TR-808 released in 1980. It was a popular instrument in early hip-hop.

SAMPLERS

Samplers capture sounds from existing music. Producers edit and pair them with original beats and melodies. This creates new songs. Many call Marley Marl the pioneer of sampling.

DECADES OF BEATS

The Roland TR-808 was only made for a few years. The beats it made are still used in trap and Southern rap.

AWARDS AND HONORS

BET AWARDS

The BET Awards began in 2001. This event honors Black entertainers. Top awards include Video of the Year and Best Female Hip Hop Artist.

MEGAN THEE STALLION

A HISTORIC WIN

Lauryn Hill won the Album of the Year Grammy in 1999. She was the first hip-hop artist to do so. She also won four other Grammys that night.

GRAMMY AWARDS

The Grammy Awards began in 1959. They award excellence in music. Hip-hop categories include Best Rap Album and Best Rap Performance. Jay-Z is one of the most-honored artists.

ROCK & ROLL HALL OF FAME

This organization was created in 1983. It honors music's greatest innovators. Hip-hop artists were first added in 2007. Rappers such as Missy Elliott and OutKast have joined since then.

TYPES OF HIP-HOP

SUGARHILL GANG

OLD SCHOOL HIP-HOP

Date Started: 1970s

Traits:

- often features live performances with DJs or bands
- beats from funk and disco music
- simple verses

Song: "Rapper's Delight" by the Sugarhill Gang

RAP ROCK

Date Started: early 1980s

Traits:

- features guitars
- blends rapping with singing
- strong, high-energy beats

Song: "It's Tricky" by Run-DMC

RUN-DMC

BLACK EYED PEAS

LL COOL J

POP HIP-HOP

Date Started: late 1980s

Traits:
- often a collaboration between artists from each genre
- combines pop with hip-hop
- mixture of sung vocals with rapped verses

Song: "Where Is the Love?" by the Black Eyed Peas

BOOM BAP

Date Started: 1980s

Traits:
- simple, raw melodies
- slower beats from jazz and soul music
- storytelling lyrics

Song: "Mama Said Knock You Out" by LL Cool J

ALTERNATIVE HIP-HOP

Date Started: late 1980s

Song: "Hey Ya!" by OutKast

Traits:

- blends hip-hop with other genres
- deep, personal songwriting
- experimental beats

2PAC

GANGSTA RAP

Date Started: mid 1980s

Traits:

- hard-hitting sound
- lyrics about street life and social issues

Song: "California Love" by 2Pac

LATIN HIP-HOP

Date Started: late 1980s

Song: "Gasolina" by Daddy Yankee

Traits:

- beats from Latin music
- features Spanish lyrics
- drum-heavy beats

DADDY YANKEE

OUTKAST

TRAP

Date Started: early 2000s

Traits:

- layered, drum-heavy production
- heavily features synthesizers and Auto-Tune
- often blends hip-hop with electronic music

Song: "BUTTERFLY EFFECT" by Travis Scott

TRAVIS SCOTT

HIP-HOP PROFILES
GRANDMASTER FLASH

Grandmaster Flash is one of hip-hop's founding fathers. His DJing helped create the genre.

TURNTABLE TALENT

Grandmaster Flash mastered the turntable at 1970s block parties. He formed Grandmaster Flash and the Furious Five in 1976. Their high-energy performances quickly became famous.

Birthday:
January 1, 1958

Hometown:
Bridgetown, Barbados

Types of Music:
old school hip-hop, funk, soul

GMF

TIMELINE

1974
Grandmaster Flash starts DJing

1976
Grandmaster Flash and the Furious Five form

1982
"The Message" is released, becoming one of early hip-hop's biggest hits

THE FURIOUS FIVE

Grandmaster Flash and the Furious Five's 1982 song "The Message" was one of hip-hop's earliest hits. *Rolling Stone* named it the greatest hip-hop song in history. In 2007, they became the first rap group to be added to the Rock & Roll Hall of Fame.

DJ PIONEER

Grandmaster Flash made DJing an art form. He laid the groundwork for early hip-hop.

QUICK MIX THEORY

Grandmaster Flash's most famous invention is the Quick Mix Theory. This uses two turntables to extend songs in a repeated loop.

HIT RELEASES

- ***The Message*** **(1982)**
- ***They Said It Couldn't Be Done*** **(1985)**
- ***The Source*** **(1986)**
- ***Ba-Dop-Boom-Bang*** **(1987)**
- ***On the Strength*** **(1988)**

2007
Grandmaster Flash and the Furious Five are added to the Rock & Roll Hall of Fame

2012
Rolling Stone **names "The Message" the greatest hip-hop song of all time**

BEASTIE BOYS

The Beastie Boys are pioneers of sampling. Their boundary-pushing music changed hip-hop's sound.

TEEN PUNK ROCKERS

The group performed punk rock as teenagers. Their experimental hip-hop songs had the most success. Their 1985 tour with Madonna gained them much attention.

Notable Members:
MCA, Mike D, Ad-Rock

Place Formed:
New York, New York

Dates Active:
1981–2012

Types of Music:
rap rock, pop hip-hop, alternative hip-hop

THE FIRST CHART-TOPPERS

The group's 1986 album *Licensed to Ill* was hip-hop's first *Billboard* 200 chart-topper. Their 1994 hit "Sabotage" was popular on MTV. They won hip-hop and alternative Grammys in 1999. They were the first artists to do this.

MILLIONS OF SALES

The group has sold millions of albums. They were added to the Rock & Rock Hall of Fame in 2012.

BEASTIE BOYS

HIT RELEASES

Licensed to Ill
(1986)

Paul's Boutique
(1989)

Ill Communication
(1994)

Hello Nasty
(1998)

To the 5 Boroughs
(2004)

TIMELINE

1985
The Beastie Boys tour with Madonna and earn mainstream attention

1987
Licensed to Ill **becomes hip-hop's first** ***Billboard*** **200 chart-topping album**

1994
"Sabotage" is released, becoming one of the Beastie Boys's most famous hits

1999
The Beastie Boys win hip-hop and alternative Grammys in one night

2012
The Beastie Boys are added to the Rock & Roll Hall of Fame

RUN-DMC

Run-DMC brought hip-hop to a wider audience. The trio became well-known for their rap rock music.

CHILDHOOD FRIENDS

Run-DMC were childhood friends. They performed in New York City clubs during the early 1980s. Their 1983 debut single "It's Like That" was a fast hit.

KINGS OF RAP ROCK

Run-DMC's *King of Rock* came out in 1985. It was the first hip-hop album with over one million sales. Their 1986 song "Walk This Way" with Aerosmith was a global hit. In 1987, they were the first hip-hop artists nominated for a Grammy.

TIMELINE

1983
Run-DMC's debut single "It's Like That" is released

1985
***King of Rock* becomes the first hip-hop album to sell over one million copies**

1986
The "Walk This Way" collaboration with Aerosmith becomes a worldwide hit

Notable Members:
Run, DMC, Jam Master Jay

Place Formed:
Queens, New York

Dates Active:
1983–2002

Types of Music:
rap rock,
pop hip-hop

QUEENS

RUN DMC

GLOBAL SUCCESS

Run-DMC have sold more than 20 million albums. They helped make hip-hop popular worldwide.

A NUMBER OF FIRSTS

Run-DMC were the first hip-hop artists with a music video on MTV. In 1986, they were the first hip-hop artists featured on the cover of *Rolling Stone*.

1987
Run-DMC become the first hip-hop artists to earn a Grammy nomination

2009
Run-DMC are added to the Rock & Roll Hall of Fame

HIT RELEASES

- ***Run-D.M.C.*** (1984)
- ***King of Rock*** (1985)
- ***Tougher Than Leather*** (1988)
- ***Down With the King*** (1993)
- ***Crown Royal*** (2001)

2PAC

2Pac is one of history's most important rappers. His poetic storytelling gave gangsta rap worldwide success.

● ART STUDENT

2Pac attended Baltimore's School for the Arts. His career began with the hip-hop group Digital Underground. He went solo in 1991.

Birthday:
June 16, 1971

Death:
September 13, 1996

Hometown:
East Harlem, New York

Types of Music:
gangsta rap,
West Coast hip-hop

HIT RELEASES

- *2Pacalypse Now* (1991)
- *Me Against the World* (1995)
- *All Eyez on Me* (1996)

FROM MUSIC TO FILM

2Pac's early albums focused on social issues. This earned them high praises. Starring roles in the movies *Juice* and *Poetic Justice* made him a household name. His 1996 album *All Eyez on Me* sold over 10 million copies. It also scored a *Billboard* Hot 100 chart-topper.

A LASTING MARK

2Pac has sold more than 75 million records. His short but purposeful career changed hip-hop.

TIMELINE

1990
2Pac joins the hip-hop group Digital Underground

1991
2Pac's debut album *2Pacalypse Now* is released

1993
2Pac stars in the hit movie *Poetic Justice* alongside Janet Jackson

1996
All Eyez on Me is released, becoming his best-selling album

2017
2Pac is added to the Rock & Roll Hall of Fame

OUTKAST

OutKast put Southern hip-hop on the map. Their bold fashions and genre-blending hits made them hip-hop icons.

BIG BOI

HIT RELEASES

- ***Southernplayalisticadillacmuzik*** **(1994)**
- ***ATLiens*** **(1996)**
- ***Aquemini*** **(1998)**
- ***Stankonia*** **(2000)**
- ***Speakerboxxx/ The Love Below*** **(2003)**

BASEMENT BEGINNING

André 3000 and Big Boi met in high school. They recorded their earliest songs in a basement studio. Their 1994 debut sold over one million copies.

GRAMMY SUCCESS

Aquemini earned OutKast their first Grammy nomination in 1999. Their 2000 song "Ms. Jackson" was their first *Billboard* Hot 100 chart-topper. Their album *Speakerboxxx/The Love Below* won 2004's Album of the Year Grammy.

TIMELINE

1992
André 3000 and Big Boi form OutKast

1994
OutKast's debut album *Southernplayalisticadillacmuzik* is released

SOUTHERN INNOVATORS

OutKast won six Grammys. They inspired a whole new generation of Southern hip-hop.

Notable Members:
André 3000, Big Boi

Place Formed:
Atlanta, Georgia

Dates Active:
1992–2007

Types of Music:
Southern hip-hop, alternative hip-hop

1999
OutKast receive their first Grammy nomination

2000
"Ms. Jackson" becomes OutKast's first *Billboard* number one hit

2004
OutKast's *Speakerboxxx/The Love Below* wins three Grammys

JAY-Z

Jay-Z is one of hip-hop's greatest songwriters and businessmen.

RAPPER AND FOUNDER

Jay-Z began rapping in the late 1980s. He started Roc-A-Fella records in 1994. His debut album *Reasonable Doubt* came out in 1996.

HIP-HOP'S FIRST BILLIONAIRE

Jay-Z's 1998 album *Vol. 2. . . Hard Knock Life* earned his first Grammy. "Empire State of Mind" came out in 2009. It was his fourth *Billboard* Hot 100 chart-topper. He became hip-hop's first billionaire in 2019.

Birthday:
December 4, 1969

Hometown:
Brooklyn, New York

Type of Music:
East Coast hip-hop

MAJOR DISCOVERIES

Jay-Z is the chairman of Roc Nation. It is an entertainment company. He helped discover Rihanna and J. Cole.

RECORD BREAKER

Jay-Z has scored 14 number one albums. He has won 25 Grammys. In 2017, he was the first rapper to be added to the Songwriters Hall of Fame.

HIT RELEASES

- *Vol. 2. . . Hard Knock Life* (1998)
- *The Blueprint* (2001)
- *The Black Album* (2003)
- *The Blueprint 3* (2009)
- *Magna Carta. . . Holy Grail* (2013)

TIMELINE

1996
Jay-Z's debut album *Reasonable Doubt* is released

1999
Jay-Z wins his first of 25 Grammys

2009
"Empire State of Mind" becomes Jay-Z's fourth *Billboard* Hot 100 number one

2017
Jay-Z is added to the Songwriters Hall of Fame

2019
Jay-Z is the first hip-hop artist to become a billionaire

MISSY ELLIOTT

Record labels overlooked female hip-hop artists for decades. Missy Elliott helped blaze new trails for female rappers.

HIT RELEASES

Supa Dupa Fly
(1997)

Miss E . . . So Addictive
(2001)

Under Construction
(2002)

This Is Not a Test!
(2003)

The Cookbook
(2005)

A HIT-MAKING PRODUCER

Elliott joined the R & B group Sista in 1991. She wrote and produced music for Aaliyah and Mariah Carey during the 1990s. Her first album *Supa Dupa Fly* came out in 1997.

TIMELINE

1997
Elliott's debut album *Supa Dupa Fly* is released

2002
Elliott wins her first Grammy

2005
"Lose Control" reaches number three on the *Billboard* Hot 100

EMINEM

A *BILLBOARD* RECORD

Eminem has won 15 Grammys. He is the first artist to have 11 *Billboard* 200 chart-topping albums.

HIT RELEASES

- ***The Slim Shady LP*** (1999)
- ***The Marshall Mathers LP*** (2000)
- ***The Eminem Show*** (2002)
- ***Recovery*** (2010)
- ***The Marshall Mathers LP 2*** (2013)

TIMELINE

1999
Eminem's debut album *The Slim Shady LP* is released

2000
The Marshall Mathers LP becomes the fastest-selling rap album

2003
"Lose Yourself" wins the Oscar for Best Original Song

2013
"The Monster" becomes Eminem's fifth *Billboard* Hot 100 number one

2022
Eminem is added to the Rock & Roll Hall of Fame

DRAKE

Drake often blends rapping with singing. He is one of the 21st century's most successful artists.

HIT RELEASES

Thank Me Later
(2010)

Nothing Was the Same
(2013)

If You're Reading This It's Too Late
(2015)

Views
(2016)

Scorpion
(2018)

TEEN ACTOR

Drake first acted on *Degrassi*: *The Next Generation* in 2001. He started recording mixtapes in 2006. His 2010 debut *Thank Me Later* became his first of 14 number one albums.

TIMELINE

2006
Drake starts recording his first mixtapes

2010
His debut album *Thank Me Later* is released

2017
Drake wins two Grammys for "Hotline Bling"

ARTIST OF THE DECADE

Drake won two Grammys for 2015's "Hotline Bling." He was named *Billboard*'s Artist of the Decade for the 2010s. In 2025, he became the first artist with 120 billion Spotify streams.

HIT AFTER HIT

Drake has more top 10 *Billboard* singles than any other artist. His 13 *Billboard* Hot 100 chart-toppers are the most of any rapper.

THE DRAKE EFFECT

Drake has worked with many up-and-coming musicians. This boosts their popularity. He has helped give artists such as The Weeknd and Bad Bunny much larger audiences.

Birthday:
October 24, 1986

Hometown:
Toronto, Canada

Types of Music:
hip-hop, R & B, pop hip-hop

2021
Drake is named *Billboard*'s Artist of the Decade for the 2010s

2025
Drake becomes the first artist with 120 billion Spotify streams

KENDRICK LAMAR

Kendrick Lamar is one of rap's greatest storytellers. He has given new life to West Coast hip-hop.

INSPIRED BY GREATNESS

Lamar started rapping as a teenager. He looked up to Jay-Z and 2Pac. Lamar first performed with the group Black Hippy. His debut album *Section.80* came out in 2011.

SOLO HEADLINER

Lamar received 11 Grammy nominations in 2016. This was a hip-hop record. In 2025, he became the first solo rapper to headline the Super Bowl Halftime Show. "Luther" became his sixth *Billboard* Hot 100 chart-topper later that year.

Birthday:
June 17, 1987

Hometown:
Compton, California

Types of Music:
West Coast hip-hop, alternative hip-hop

HIT RELEASES

- ***Section.80*** (2011)
- ***good kid, m.A.A.d city*** (2012)
- ***To Pimp a Butterfly*** (2015)
- ***Mr. Morale & the Big Steppers*** (2022)
- ***GNX*** (2024)

PULITZER WINNER

Lamar is the only rapper to win a Pulitzer Prize. He has won over 25 Grammys. He has won more Grammys than any other rapper.

THE HIGHEST PRAISES

Lamar's albums have received higher overall critic scores than any other hip-hop artist.

TIMELINE

2013
Lamar receives seven Grammy nominations

2015
President Barack Obama names "How Much a Dollar Cost" his favorite song of the year

2016
Lamar receives 11 Grammy nominations, a hip-hop record

2018
Lamar becomes the first hip-hop artist to win a Pulitzer Prize

2025
Lamar becomes the first solo rapper to headline the Super Bowl Halftime show

MEGAN THEE STALLION

Megan Thee Stallion is an award-winning rapper. She is known for her viral songs and empowering lyrics.

IN THE FAMILY

Megan Thee Stallion's mother was a rapper. This inspired Megan Thee Stallion. She released her first song in 2016.

Birthday:
February 15, 1995

Hometown:
San Antonio, Texas

Types of Music:
trap, pop hip-hop

GOING VIRAL

In 2020, she released the song "Savage" with Beyoncé. It was Megan Thee Stallion's first song to top the *Billboard* Hot 100 chart. In 2021, she won two Grammys for it. She also won the Grammy for Best New Artist.

HIT RELEASES

Good News (2020)

Traumazine (2022)

Megan (2024)

Megan: Act II (2024)

AWARD WINNER

She has won four MTV Video Music Awards. She has also won five BET Awards.

TIMELINE

2016
Megan Thee Stallion releases her first song

2020
"Savage" is Megan Thee Stallion's first song to reach the *Billboard* Hot 100 chart

2021
Megan Thee Stallion wins her first three Grammys

2022
Megan Thee Stallion wins her second *Billboard* Music Award

2025
"Hiss" becomes Megan Thee Stallion's third number one hit on the *Billboard* Hot 100 chart

BAD BUNNY

Bad Bunny is one of music's most-streamed artists. He has brought Latin hip-hop and trap to global audiences.

COLLEGE HITMAKER

Bad Bunny listened to reggaeton growing up. In college, he recorded music that became popular online. His 2016 debut single "Soy Peor" was an instant hit.

THE MOST-STREAMED

In 2020, *El Último Tour Del Mundo* was the first all-Spanish *Billboard* 200 chart-topper. Bad Bunny was Spotify's most-streamed artist in 2020, 2021, 2022, and 2025. In 2026, he became the Super Bowl Halftime Show's first solo Latin performer.

TIMELINE

2016
Bad Bunny's debut single "Soy Peor" is an instant hit

2020
***El Último Tour Del Mundo* becomes the first all-Spanish album to top the *Billboard* 200**

2021
Bad Bunny wins his first Grammy

LATIN PIONEER

Bad Bunny has proved that artists can achieve worldwide success without performing in English.

HIT RELEASES

X 100PRE
(2018)

El Último Tour Del Mundo
(2020)

Un Verano Sin Ti
(2022)

Nadie Sabe Lo Que Va a Pasar Mañana
(2023)

DeBÍ TiRAR MáS FOToS
(2025)

Birthday:
March 10, 1994

Hometown:
San Juan, Puerto Rico

Types of Music:
Latin hip-hop, trap

SAN JUAN

2022
Bad Bunny is named Spotify's most-streamed artist for the third straight year

2026
Bad Bunny wins three Grammys and later becomes the first solo Latin artist to headline the Super Bowl Halftime Show

THE FUTURE OF HIP-HOP

DON TOLIVER

Modern hip-hop often uses Digital Audio Workstations. These help artists make beats and samples outside of expensive studios. TikTok has allowed Lil Nas X and Jack Harlow to gain viral fame quickly.

LIL NAS X

JACK HARLOW

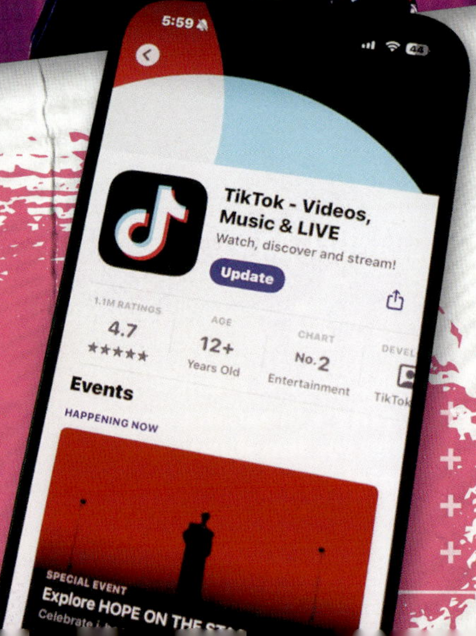

Anuel AA and Ozuna have kept Latin hip-hop popular worldwide. Don Toliver and Lil Baby have changed trap in new ways. Cardi B and Doechii have made female rappers more popular. Hip-hop has a rich history. Its future remains bright thanks to these artists!

GLOSSARY

alternative—related to something different and typically outside of the mainstream

Auto-Tune—an electronic instrument that can edit and change an artist's vocals

breakdancing—an energetic type of dancing that features special footwork and athletic movements

collaboration—something created while working with others

culture—the beliefs, arts, and ways of life in a place or society

debut—first appearance

Digital Audio Workstations—computer programs that allow vocals to be recorded and beats to be made using the same device

freestyle—a hip-hop style where artists make up a song's lyrics as they perform

generation—a group of people who were born around the same time

genre—a category for a type of music

innovators—people who create new ideas and techniques or who positively change existing ones

inspired—gave someone an idea about what to do or create

mainstream—common and shared by a large audience

melodies—series of lyrics and sounds that are arranged with a rhythm

mixtapes—collections of songs, usually released for free by artists

nominated—chosen as a candidate for an award

Oscar—a yearly award presented for achievements in film; Oscars are also called Academy Awards.

Pulitzer Prize—an award that recognizes journalism and art that have greatly impacted society

reggaeton—a Latin music genre that combines reggae and dance music with hip-hop

rhythms—repeated patterns of movement or sound

samples—lyrics or beats taken from existing songs that are reworked and edited into new music

subgenres—smaller, more specific types of music within a genre

synthesizers—electronic musical instruments that can create sounds and change existing sounds

turntables—circular, rotating musical instruments that allow DJs to play and edit records

viral—popular from being shared quickly

WRITE ABOUT IT!

- Which artist do you think has had the biggest impact on hip-hop? **Why?**
- What are some of your favorite hip-hop songs? **Why do you like them?**
- How do you think hip-hop music will continue to **change** in the future?

ALSO CHECK OUT

INDEX

alternative hip-hop, 18, 22, 29, 38
Bad Bunny, 5, 9, 11, 37, 42–43
Beastie Boys, 7, 10, 22–23
BET Awards, 14, 41
Billboard charts, 23, 27, 28, 29, 30, 31, 32, 34, 35, 37, 38, 40, 41, 42
boom bap, 5, 17
Drake, 4, 5, 9, 11, 36–37
Elliott, Missy, 15, 32–33
Eminem, 11, 34–35
gangsta rap, 8, 18, 26
Grammys, 8, 10, 15, 23, 24, 25, 28, 29, 30, 31, 32, 33, 34, 35, 36, 37, 38, 39, 40, 41, 42, 43
Grandmaster Flash, 20–21
Jay-Z, 15, 30–31, 38
Lamar, Kendrick, 5, 11, 38–39
Latin hip-hop, 5, 11, 19, 42, 43, 45
Megan Thee Stallion, 14, 40–41
MTV, 23, 25, 33, 41
old school hip-hop, 16, 20
Oscar, 11, 34, 35
OutKast, 9, 15, 18, 19, 28–29
pop hip-hop, 5, 17, 22, 25, 33, 34, 37, 40
rap rock, 7, 16, 22, 24, 25, 34
Rock & Roll Hall of Fame, 15, 21, 23, 25, 27, 33, 35
Run-DMC, 7, 10, 16, 24–25
Songwriters Hall of Fame, 31, 33
Spotify, 37, 42, 43
Super Bowl Halftime Show, 38, 39, 42, 43
2Pac, 18, 26–27, 38
trap, 5, 9, 13, 19, 40, 42, 43, 45

The images in this book are reproduced through the courtesy of: Gorodenkoff, front cover (hero, DJ), p. 4 (top left); Mauro Rodrigues, front covers (hype man); Tiler84, front cover (mixer controller); Kevin Winter/ Staff/ Getty Images, pp. 3 (Megan Thee Stallion), 15 (top right), 41 (Megan Thee Stallion); Nikola Spasenoski, pp. 3 (Missy Elliott), 33 (Missy Elliott); Jgphotographydetroit, pp. 3 (Eminem), 10 (Drake), 34-35 (Eminem), 37 (middle), 45 (middle left); Monostereo 88, p. 4 (top right); Joseph Okpako/ Contributor/ Getty Images, p. 4 (Drake); Anthony Barboza/ Contributor/ Getty Images, pp. 4 (bottom right), 16 (Sugarhill Gang); Biloxi Sun Herald/ Contributor/ Getty Images, pp. 4-5; Mehaniq, p. 5 (top left); Christopher Polk/ Contributor/ Getty Images, pp. 5 (Bad Bunny), 38 (right); Mika Väisänen/ Wikimedia Commons, p. 6 (DJ Cool Herc); EQRoy, p. 6 (right); David Redfern/ Staff/ Getty Images, p. 7 (Beastie Boys); Michael Ochs Archives/ Stringer/ Getty Images, pp. 7 (Run-DMC), 13 (bottom), 16 (Run-DMC), 24 (middle), 25 (top left); Al Pereira/ Contributor/ Getty Images, pp. 8 (Queen Latifah), 26 (top); Jeff Kravitz/ Contributor/ Getty Images, pp. 8 (Lil' Kim), 35 (middle); David Corio/ Contributor/ Getty Images, pp. 8 (bottom), 12; Frank Micelotta Archive/ Contributor/ Getty Images, pp. 9-10; Raymond Boyd/ Contributor/ Getty Images, pp. 10 (Outkast), 18 (2Pac), 27 (middle, bottom); PYMCA/ Avalon/ Contributor/ Getty Images, p. 10 (DJ Cool Herc); Vinyls/ Alamy Stock Photo, p. 10 (1979); Bernd Schwabe/ Wikimedia Commons, pp. 10 (grammy), 23 (grammy), 25 (grammy), 29 (grammy), 31 (grammy), 32 (grammy), 36 (grammy), 39 (grammy), 41 (grammy), 42 (grammy); MediaPunc Inc/ Alamy Stock Photo, pp. 10 (Rum-DMC with Areosmith), 26 (middle); Featureflash Photo Agency, pp. 11 (Eminem), 15 (top left), 29 (middle left), 30 (top), 32 (top), 40 (top right); RGR Collection/ Alamy Stock Photo, p. 11 (1990s); Steve Sykes, p. 11 (Lil Wayne); Adam McCullough, pp. 11 (2018), 37 (top right); DFree, pp. 11 (Bad Bunny), 22 (bottom left); 32bitmaschine/ Wikimedia Commons, p. 12 (turntable); Future Music/ Contributor/ Getty Images, p. 13 (top); Joho345/ Wikimedia Commons, p. 13 (middle left); fr4dd/ Wikimedia Commons, p. 13 (middle right); ZUMA Press, Inc./ Alamy Stock Photo, p. 14 (top); Paras Griffin/ Stringer/ Getty Images, p. 14 (Megan Thee Stallion); Emma McIntyre/ Staff/ Getty Images, p. 15 (bottom left); Amy Sussman/ Staff/ Getty Images, p. 15 (bottor right); Paul Natkin/ Contributor/ Getty Images, p. 17 (LL Cool J); KMazur/ Contributor/ Getty Images, p. 17 (Black Eyed Peas); Tim P. Whitby/ Stringer/ Getty Images, pp. 18-19 (Outkast); Florencia Tan Jun/ Stringer/ Getty Images, p. 19 (Daddy Yankee); Mauricio Santana/ Contributor/ Getty Images, p. 19 (Travis Scott); Mika-photography/ Wikimedia Commons, p. 20 (top); A. Jamal, p. 20 (middle left); Manuela Schueler, p. 20 (middle right); lev radin, pp. 20 (bottom right), 45 (top); Victor Frankowski/ Southbank Centre Wikimedia Commons, p. 21 (left); 3DMI, pp. 21 (2007), 23 (2012) 25 (2009), 27 (2017), 33 (2023), 35 (2022), 41 (2022); Variety/ Contributor/ Getty Images, p. 21 (middle); Sugar Hill Records/ Wikimedia Commons, p. 21 (top); Karsten.mcvay/ Wikimedia Commons, p. 22 (top); Ron Galella, Ltd./ Contributor/ Getty Images, p. 22 (middle); Tierney, pp. 22 (New York), 25 (top right), 30 (botto right); bakameh/ Wikimedia Commons, p. 23 (top); Theo Wargo/ Staff/ Getty Images, pp. 23 (middle), 42-43; Def Jam Recordings/ Wikimedia Commons, p. 23 (logo); agwilson, p. 23 (bottom); Luigi Novi/ Wikimedia Commons, p. 24 (top); Profile Records/ Wikipedia Commons, p. 25 (logo); Jeff Pinilla/ Wikimedia Commons, p. 25 (middle); Tim Mosenfelder/ Contributor/ Getty Images, p. 26 (bottor left); James, p. 26 (bottom right); Photo 12/ Alamy Stock Photo, p. 27 (top); Sterling Munksgard, p. 28 (left, right); Kathy Hutchins, pp. 29 (top left), 37 (bottom 2021), 39 (middle), 40 (bottom); Gregory Bojorquez/ Contributor/ Getty Images, p. 29 (right); Alessi p. 29 (middle right); Adam J. Sablich, p. 30 (middle); landmarkmedi p. 30 (bottom left); Debby Wong, p. 31 (top, middle); Everett Collection, pp. 31 (bottom), 33 (middle), 34 (top left); Ronald Siemoneit/ Contributor/ Getty Images, p. 32 (middle); Christopher Boswell, p. 33 (middle left); Marcin Kadziolka, p. 33 (middle right); WFDJ_Stock, p. 33 (2019); DOD News Features/ Wikimedia Commons, p. 34 (top right, middle left); John Gunion/ Contributor/ Getty Images, p. 34 (middle right); Brian Rasic/ Contributor/ Getty Images, p. 34 (bottom left); D. Summers, p. 34 (bottom right); The Come Up Show/ Wikimedia Commons, p. 36 (top); David Livingstor Contributor/ Getty Images, p. 36 (middle); Denise Truscello/ Contributor/ Getty Images, p. 37 (top left); Diego Thomazini, p. 37 (bottom 2025); eranda, p. 37 (bottom right); Kobby Dagan, p. 38 (left); Samir Hussein/ Contributor/ Getty Images, p. 38 (botton left); Underawesternsky, p. 38 (bottom right); Christian Bertrand, pp. 39 (top), 45 (bottom left); CBS Photo Archive/ Contributor/ Gett Images, p. 39 (bottom); ADWEEK/ Wikimedia Commons, p. 40 (top left); L Paul Mann, p. 40 (middle left); Megan Varner/ Stringer/ Gett Images, p. 40 (middle); Jin, p. 40 (middle right); Eduardo Manurae, p. 43 (top); Michael Loccisano/ Staff/ Getty Images, p. 43 (middle); Alexander Tamargo/ Contributor/ Getty Images, p. 43 (bottom left); Martin, p. 43 (bottom right); Franklin Sheard Jr, p. 44 (top); John Shearer/ MTV VMAs 2021/ Contributor/ Getty Images, p. 44 (middle); Pressmaster, p. 44 (bottom left); Bendix M, p. 44 (bottom right); Ivanhoe Garibay, p. 45 (middle right); Katie Flores/ Contributor/ Getty Images, p. 45 (bottom right).